CU00866920

INTENTIONAL
HAPPINESS

INTENTIONAL HAPPINESS

The Life-Changing Guide To
Being Happy and Staying Happy

JULIE LEONARD

INTENTIONAL HAPPINESS: The Life-Changing Guide To Being Happy and Staying Happy

Copyright © Julie Leonard 2020

To Leonardo, my Why in everything I do. I love you.

'Consciously and deliberately choose
to pursue an Intentionally Happy Life.
Be proactive, not reactive, and cultivate
a life of joy and fulfillment.'

Julie x

CONTENTS

PREFACE

In 2019 I was at an event in Bucharest with an incredible lineup of speakers. From that weekend away, some big shifts happened for me, one of which is how I became the Happiness Evangelist.

One of the speakers was Guy Kawasaki, Brand Evangelist. Oh, that word irked me. Evangelist. Sounds religious. But it stuck in my head. I kept thinking about it. During the weekend, my good friend and colleague Ginny and I were dreaming big as we always do. Talking about when we walk out on stage as speakers, experts in our field. I was thinking of other names for 'expert'. Another speaker and author I follow is a Kindness Tsar and I was thinking of what title I could give myself. I kept coming back to this word Evangelist. And surprisingly, after a few weeks, I settled on Happiness Evangelist.

I wanted to claim the word and make it my own. To spread the message that you can change, you can be proactive, you can take charge of your happiness. I liked the idea of spreading the word. I feel so strongly that people need to know that you don't have to settle. That it's not 'just who I am' or feel stuck believing that you can't change. Or that it can't happen for you or you are not reaching anywhere near your full potential. I'm all about truly living, not merely existing. Not settling for fine but striving for amazing. And so I took on the title of Happiness Evangelist along with Life Coach.

Two years ago I was also approached to create a goal-setting / accountability group. I loved the idea and as I worked on developing and mapping it out, it began to evolve into something more. I have been drawn for a long time to living with intention and felt this was a good fit with goal setting. So I launched the Intentional Living Group. This evolved over time into a 12-month Intentional Happiness Course which became my online Intentional Happiness Circle and inspired this book.

In this book, I share some concepts and research on happiness, what makes us happy, and how we can take control of our happiness. I share chapter by chapter the stages you can take to cultivate your own life of living with intention. We will go on the journey together and I will guide you step by step towards a proactive life of purpose. Imagine how that will feel, to have clarity on what is important in your life. To be clear on your goals and to be free of the things that distract you from what is important to you. To know that every single day you are living the life you truly desire and clearly and consciously moving forwards with your life goals.

This is what you will have by the end of this book. I give you clear steps and exercises to implement in your life. I've combined my 30+ years of experience, the feedback from the Intentional Happiness Courses I have run and the research behind the concepts and why they work. I highly recommend following the steps in the order that they appear in the book. But you can also dip into each chapter as they stand alone too or if you feel there is a particular topic that calls to you at a particular time. Each chapter has exercises for you to complete to cement your knowledge and help you move concretely forwards. Please take the proper time to complete the exercises before moving on. Some may be quicker and easier to complete (no zero days and accountability). Others may take much longer (such as decluttering and values). Taking a little time now will reap enormous benefits in the long run.

So here I am. Julie Leonard. Happiness Evangelist and Life Coach, passionate about living an Intentionally Happy Life. With a strong drive to share my energy, positivity, tools, and knowledge with you in order for you to live a truly happy, fulfilling, and intentional life.

INTRODUCTION
(AND MY STORY)

I grew up in Scotland where, particularly for men, emotions are not generally spoken about. My father, now in his 80's, has been depressed my whole life. But it was never discussed and I never understood, growing up, that there was anything wrong with him. My parents are both loving, good people who wanted only but the best for me. They didn't do anything overtly 'bad', but through my dad's illness and his behaviour, I internalised a lot of negative thoughts. My father was often in his own head. We would sit at the dinner table and when I was talking to him, often he would either ignore me or cut across my conversation. He didn't do it deliberately, he was just so caught up in his own thoughts. But I interpreted this as something about me. As a result, as a child and teenager, and even into my 20's, I was an anxious person. I was a worrier, sensitive, and with very little self-esteem. I never felt good enough, or that my opinion counted and I truly believed I was the ugliest woman in the world.

At school, I was shy and was bullied and picked upon. I wasn't popular and I felt like I didn't fit in. At University I realised I wasn't completely weird, found my best friend but still struggled with anxiety and low confidence. I couldn't even walk into the cafeteria on my own. I was so nervous. It's probably no surprise that I chose to study Psychology. I had to work out what was going on in my own head!

My negative thoughts had a huge impact on the choices I made, my relationships, and how happy I felt. My happiness went up and down like a rollercoaster as it was based on external influences. I didn't have the confidence or self-esteem, or indeed the resilience, to feel happy in myself. I often thought 'If I was more beautiful I would be happy/popular/loved/successful'.

When my long-term and very negative relationship came to an end in my early 30's, I finally had the time, space, and tools to transform myself and my life. My personal life wasn't so great but professionally I was doing very well. All this anxiety and negative thinking meant that I was empathic and compassionate and identified with many of the women I supported. I'd worked my way up to becoming the manager of a mental health organisation and felt I had a career that gave me such meaning and purpose.

I remember clearly sitting on my sofa one day. I was low in

mood, emotionally exhausted and feeling alone. I was confident in my job (supporting women to make positive changes in their lives!) and had advanced in my career. But apart from work, I felt I had nothing and was unhappy and unfulfilled in my life. It was then, sitting on my sofa, that I had a moment that changed my life. I asked myself *'What is more scary? Staying as I am or facing my fears and putting myself out there?'*

And the realisation was that **I was more scared to stay in the life I had. To remain stuck and unfulfilled.**

AND SO I BEGAN MY TRANSFORMATION.

It took a while but here I am. I found love with a wonderful Italian man, changed everything in my life and moved from Scotland to Germany. I have a beautiful son and I am a successful Certified Life Coach. From the shy girl who couldn't speak out in class, I now run seminars and courses. I am a regular podcast guest and I even speak at international events!

With all of this experience, I have gained empathy, compassion and understanding of the struggles people face. And I am passionate about sharing my skills, knowledge and tools with you. I can't wait to support you to transform yourself and to transform your life.

LIVE TO YOUR FULL POTENTIAL. I DID IT AND SO CAN YOU!

PART 1

CHAPTER 1

WHAT IS HAPPINESS?

For over 20 years I worked for mental health services in Scotland. I loved it. Even though my dream had been to be a psychologist, I quickly revised that when I saw the direct impact I could have on people through the work I was doing. What I liked most was that I could go and see people in their homes, in their own environment. I loved that I could spend quality time with people and really get to know them. Each hour was different, every person and their story unique.

What most people shared with me was this. When I asked them what they wanted, what their goals in life were, what recovery meant to them, almost all of the time they said: 'I want to be happy.'

This started me on my journey to find out more about happiness and what happiness means to people. I would ask them, what do we need to change to be happy. And we would break it down into social, emotional and practical goals and then break that down further into actionable steps. We didn't call it coaching but it's exactly what we were doing together.

And you know, what people wanted in order to be happy, wasn't lots of money, or a big house or more material goods. They wanted to make connections, to build friendships and not feel so isolated. They wanted to find meaning and purpose. They wanted a reason to get up every morning. They wanted to be free of negative thoughts and limiting beliefs. They wanted to feel confident and have higher levels of self-esteem. Many said they wanted 'peace and quiet and peace of mind'. All attainable. All possible. They just needed someone to support them, to believe in them and to work alongside them on their journey.

When I then moved to Germany, I was clear I still wanted to work with women to support them to transform themselves and their lives. It felt like such a natural continuation to become a Life Coach. I created my Coaching business and coach women all over the world to change their negative thinking, get clarity on what they want and to achieve their dreams.

When I moved to Germany I also wanted to create a group to connect expat women together. The kind of group I would like to attend and which would provide some meaningful discussion and connection. So I created the Happiness Club. I based it on an idea from Psychologies magazine of creating a group, similar to a book club, to discuss aspects of happiness. I created a slightly larger group and each month we discussed a topic related to happiness. Some months we discussed the keys to happiness as researched by the organisation Action for Happiness. Other months I introduced topics based on my years of working with clients or something I had read that had piqued my interest.

I started that group back in 2014 and it has now evolved into my online International Women's Happiness Club. Again, there are recurring themes around happiness that are universal, no matter where women join me from; meaningful connections, relationships, love, a sense of purpose, a feeling of balance (inner and outer), feeling calm, a realisation that materialism isn't the sole answer to happiness, health is important, goal setting and support. And month on month, year on year, my group attracts more and more women seeking a more balanced, healthy and joyful life.

And what I have seen first-hand over the past 4 decades is backed up by research. Now, more than ever, we need to find the tools and support to feel happier. The World Happiness Report, funded by the UN, shows that despite higher standards of living, Americans report that they are unhappier now than they were 20-30 years ago. This is also reflected in the increased use of prescriptions for antidepressants. The CDC has reported that there was a 65% increase in the use of antidepressants during a time frame of 15 years.

Of course, money is essential for living and we need and want some material goods in our life. But that is insufficient for happiness. And hundreds of research studies in most countries in the world support this. Money buys some happiness and research has shown a positive relationship between money and well-being: better physical health, better academic success, less stressful life events and better mental health. When we are financially poor, money equates more to happiness but as we grow richer, that reduces. Kahneman and Deaton calculated in 2010 that the amount of money we need to earn before its correlation with happiness diminishes is only $75,000. Let's not forget that not all happiness requires money.

We know from research that money isn't the only thing that makes people happy. Happiness comes more from internal happiness than from external material possessions. Action for Happiness did some research into what makes people happy and found that there are 10 keys to happiness including relationships and connection, meaning and purpose, exercise, doing things for others and resilience.

And although a state of happiness is subjective and differs from person to person, the good news is that you can increase your own personal happiness. This is why I have created this step-by-step guide to achieving, and maintaining, happiness. How to be Intentionally Happy.

THE RIPPLE EFFECT OF HAPPINESS

There is plenty of evidence that being happy is good for you. Apart from the obvious that feeling happy feels good, research shows that it has physical and psychological health benefits, promotes career success and benefits social connections. And it has a ripple effect. When you are happy, living the life you want you feel positive and purposeful. You feel balanced and calm, excited and anticipating great things. All this affects those around you. Your partner, children, friends and colleagues all benefit. As do those in your outer circle - neighbours, store workers, the bus driver and other complete strangers you encounter. When you radiate happiness, you touch many lives, known and unknown. And there is a ripple effect on yourself. Research shows that happiness adds years to your life. You feel more joy every day and in what you do, you have better career success, deeper and more fulfilling relationships and much more.

SLOWING DOWN THE HEDONIC TREADMILL

People are now also realising that happiness is more of an internal feeling rather than a result of owning more stuff. We've all experienced the relative short-lived happiness after some retail therapy. This quick feeling of happiness then falls back to our set-point happiness. Research shows that we all have our individual happiness set point that we return to once that fleeting feeling of increased happiness fades. This reversal back to a set-point happiness level has been named the Hedonic Adaptation, or Hedonic Treadmill. It basically means that we have to continually seek out new stuff, often by buying more things, in order to lift our happiness levels.

Hedonic Adaptation is what makes humans so adaptable to difficult situations, which is very useful to us. But it also means that positive events quickly become the new 'normal'. Some say that the pursuit of happiness is like being on a treadmill, that you constantly have to feed yourself with positive emotions to stay happy.

Research by Positive Psychologist, Sonja Lyubomirsky, shows that everyone's happiness set-point is about 50% genetic and 10% circumstantial. Most importantly though, 40% of this set-point is influenced by our thoughts, actions and attitudes. The default happiness set-point is also shown as being above neutral, so leaning towards being positive. This is a great starting point for us!

It means that your happiness level is not set in stone and that happiness can actively be pursued. We can increase our happiness set-point and use some tools to slow down the hedonic adaptation and intentionally cultivate happiness in our lives.

Happiness is important to people across the world. In many cultures, we have traditionally been told that money and materialism will make us happy. What we do know is that those things give us short term happiness, fleeting happiness. What we want to do is create long-lasting happiness that is intentional and resilient.

What that looks like varies from person to person and is very subjective. I'm all about creating a tool kit of happiness. The resources we need at different points of the day, the week, the year. Your happiness toolkit may include such things as a gratitude practice, meditation, journaling, exercise or reading.

WHAT HAPPINESS MEANS TO ME

For me, happiness is having resilience and finding balance in my life. It is finding joy each day.

People often think I live in some kind of happiness bubble.

That I'm happy and smiling all the time. I smile a lot. And I'm a happy and positive person. But I'm also human. And life happens, even to Life Coaches! I have days when I feel hurt, or angry or disappointed. Where I catch myself having negative thoughts or ruminating on something someone said. Or finding myself spiraling down with a negative thought.

Happiness for me is that I have a core inner strength, a resilience that means that I can bounce back from tough times. That I can feel negative emotions and have negative thoughts but can pull myself back quickly. I have learned the tools that build and maintain my resilience and that I can access when I need them or use them every day.

I truly believe we can cultivate happiness. That it's not a fixed point. That by taking intentional and proactive action you can nurture and grow your happiness as well as maintain it, just like a garden. You need good foundations, a clear vision, and a plan for what it should look like. And you must do a little every day to maintain and grow it.

So let's begin by getting clear on what makes you happy by looking at how happy you are now.

CHAPTER 2

HOW HAPPY ARE YOU?

A good starting point in the pursuit of happiness is to know how happy you are right now. I've made it easy for you. Head over to my website and take my Happiness Quiz: http://julieleonardcoaching.com/happiness-quiz/

From the quiz, you will get a happiness score. It gives you a happiness baseline that you can work on. You'll also get a bonus 'wheel of life' colouring sheet, to mindfully colour in. This will give you a visual representation of how happy your life is right now and which areas of your life need work.

Now let's go on with these exercises to explore more deeply how happy you are.

EXERCISE 1

Get a notepad and pen. What word comes to mind when you think of your life? Take a few minutes to sit with this question and be open to the words that come to mind. Write them down.

EXERCISE 2

Next, here are some good reflective questions to ask yourself. Write down the answers.

1. What in your life currently brings you joy, makes you happy, gets you bounding out of bed, makes you smile?
2. What kind of people are you surrounded by? Are they positive, supportive people who are your mini cheerleading squad?
3. How much do you find yourself moaning and complaining? If you keep complaining, it may help to vent but it only reinforces and focuses on the negative. Of course, there may be big stuff going on for you. What can you change? If you can't change it, how can you change how you respond to it?
4. Is your life where you thought it would be now?
5. What are you most grateful for?
6. What are you most proud of?
7. What projects have you started but never finished?
8. What stresses you out the most at the moment?
9. What's the one thing you would like to be remembered for?

10. What word sums up your last year?

You now have a better understanding of how happy you are and a baseline from which to work from.

CHAPTER 3

HAPPINESS IS IN YOUR CONTROL

So now choose a word for this year. My word this year is JOY. And what I intentionally do is work on the things that bring me joy. I even created an Intentional Happiness Mood Board (more on that later).

Happiness is so much in your control. The research by Sonja Lyubomirsky tells us that at least 50% of it is in our control. Nothing is permanent. Nothing is fixed. *You* can change. *Your life* can change and you can take so much *control* over the direction you wish your life to take.

With everything in life, it's important to focus on what you can control, not on what you can't. And realise that you can either change the things you can or change how you respond to things.

Make happiness your goal.

Choose to be happy.

Change beliefs and negative thinking, smile, learn new skills and be around positive people. Be conscious, be intentional. Not everyone is happy simply because of their personality.

Happy people choose to be happy and work at it.

For example, as you read in the introduction. I grew up shy and introverted with lots of negative thoughts and quite a worrier. Hugely affected by my upbringing, I could have remained that way. But I made a conscious decision to be different and have worked so hard on myself to have come this far in my journey.

Happiness has a set point, but research says we can reset it. More than 50% is in our control, so it's a choice about how happy we want to be. I definitely believe my happiness set point is much higher now, especially through using mindfulness and self-compassion.

I really like this quote from Psychologist William James. *'The greatest discovery of any generation is that a human can alter his life by altering his attitude'*. By adopting a positive and proactive attitude you can change your life.

If you do the same things every day, you are going to get the same results. Or as Albert Einstein is widely credited as saying:

'The definition of insanity is doing the same thing over and over again, but expecting different results". Taking control, being conscious of what you want, and making positive changes will take you forwards into the life you want. Stop comparing yourself to others and choose what happiness means to you and what things you want in life that will make you truly happy. It's your life, no one else's. Think only of what is important and a priority to you.

The research of Sonja Luybomirsky is now said to be oversimplified and even Sonja herself agrees that it's a simplified pie chart. But the essence is there. An optimistic, hopeful message that so much of our happiness, our life ahead of us, can be shaped by us. That so much of our happiness is in our control.

The science of Neuroplasticity also confirms this. We can change our brains. Not only have I seen it in myself and in the 1000+ women I have worked with over the years, but science tells us that the brain is not fixed, that we can rewire it. We can train it just like we train our bodies. In 2004 scientists gathered at the Dalai Lama's home in Dharamsala, India to compare the brains of novice meditators and the Buddhist monks who had meditated for more than 10,000 hours. What they discovered was the Buddhist monks had a very enlarged left prefrontal cortex (the site of positive emotions including happiness) and that activity in this area overshadowed activity in the right prefrontal cortex (the site of negative emotions and anxiety). You don't need to be meditating to the same extent as the monks, but what this highlights is that in choosing the right tools and consciously focusing on your happiness you can change the structure of your brain so that you increase your positivity and happiness.

Having consistency and commitment to the process is essential. This will yield long-lasting not fleeting happiness. We are building healthy habits and focus.

Define your own happiness.

Let yourself be happy. Give yourself permission to be happy. And let's become intentional.

CHAPTER 4

WHAT IS INTENTIONAL HAPPINESS?

Many years ago I was at a place in my life where I had choices to make. My long term relationship had ended. It had been a difficult and toxic relationship for many years. When it ended I was full of fear about what I wanted to do in my life and what I could do. Even believing that I was capable of doing some of the most simple and fun things (such as going out for a drink or going on holiday) made me fearful. As I mentioned in the Introduction I decided to face my fears and go for it! I've always believed you have one life and you must live it to the max.

Don't settle for fine.

Strive for amazing!

It's well documented that the biggest regret dying people have is that they didn't live a life true to themselves. And it's not just limited to those who are at the end of their life. When I worked in Glasgow, time and time again I saw people existing and not living. People without hope, without meaning and purpose, without direction, without the belief that they are more than this and that they deserve more.

Over all the years I have worked, especially in my coaching practice, I've seen so many women who felt that they have lost time, missed out on so much or wasted time. My clients feel that they are not living a truly authentic life. I feel my life's purpose is to help as many people as possible to live the life they want to live.

So after my breakup and at this major turning point in my life, I went for it. I said Yes! to everything. So much so, a close friend once joked I'd 'go to the opening of an envelope!'. And I tell you, I had so much fun! I had some incredible experiences, and some not so great ones, but mostly great adventures. The first year I had 10 holidays. I travelled so much! I went to concerts, the theatre and parties. I was even a roadie for friends supporting a well-known band on their UK tour. And I am so thankful for all of it.

Because I said Yes to things I ended up being the plus one for my close friend Wendy, at a wedding in Romania where I met my wonderful Italian man. I moved to Munich, Germany to be with him (something else I said Yes to) and now have a beautiful son and run my own company.

I realised after a while that saying yes to everything brought me so much of what I wanted. It brings possibilities, but it just might not be the ones you want. That's when I realised being intentional was even more important. Being focused and clear on what is actually important to me. And, by taking away all the things I think I *should* do or *ought* to do, I could be more intentional on what I needed to do to create the life I desired.

So all of my achievements have not just been down to luck but down to clarity, focus and being proactive, not reactive. It's down to really hard work and intentionally and consciously working towards goals that are truly important to me. I've had to prioritise and be clear on what I want in life and not get caught up in all the things that don't add to that or simply detract from it. Things I don't need to do or want to do. So opening up and saying yes to more may be part of your journey forwards. But also learning to say No and focusing on what you have prioritised, will take you in the direction of living an Intentionally Happy life.

I created the term Intentional Happiness to capture all that we have already spoken about. That happiness is within our control, and that we have the ability to create the life we want.

If we just get intentional about it. It's taking control and taking goal setting a step further. It's consciously and deliberately doing things every day towards the things that you prioritise. It's focusing on what's important and not wasting time on things that don't matter so much.

This reminds me of my client Elizabeth. We were working on an asset map for her. An asset map is taking a big piece of paper and making a visual picture of someone's life. In this situation, we were mapping out all the people in her life. This is an especially useful tool when someone is depressed or struggling with negative thoughts and feels alone.

We put her in the middle and created rings around her that went further away from her. In these rings, we mapped out the people in her life and how close she was to them. As we went through the exercise one thing stood out. She had a lot of people in her life. Yet the people she regularly spent time with left her feeling more negative and disconnected than before she met up with them. On the other hand, she had a group of girlfriends who were genuine, caring and so much fun to be around. She lit up when she spoke about them.

When I asked her why she rarely saw them her reply was: 'I don't have time'. Elizabeth was caught up seeing people that made her feel worse, not better and had no time to see the positive people in her life. Being intentional would mean asking yourself why you spend time with each person. What you get from them and who you really want to spend time with and therefore prioritising them in your life. And this was what I worked on with Elizabeth. To be intentional about her friendships. To prioritise and spend her precious time with people who made her feel amazing.

For all of us, life is extremely busy. We can easily get caught up in the day to day, getting through the week. Before you know it, the weeks and months have flown by. I spent my 20's and 30's busy living life but it wasn't until my late 30's that I discovered Intentional Living. I found a way to focus on what I want in life and to live with more intention and purpose. To work every single day to live intentionally the life I really want to live. Being *proactive,* not reactive in my life.

Living an Intentional Life means:

Every single day **consciously** doing the things that are important to me.

Focusing on only the most important aspects of my life.

Prioritizing what is truly important.

Being *proactive,* not reactive in my life.

Being clear on my **values** and how I want to live my life.

Being **clear** on who I want in my life.

And **what** I want in my life.

Being clear on the **lifestyle** I wish to lead.

Having **clarity** and specific **goals** and working towards what it is exactly I want.

Setting **boundaries.**

Living with **integrity.**

Slowing down.

Feeling **aligned.**

Regularly asking myself **WHY?** And being happy with the answer or changing direction.

It's an **ongoing process**. It is actively working towards the life I wish to lead.

In 2014, I packed up my life and moved to Munich, Germany. I'm a Life Coach so of course, I created a (simple) vision board and got clear on my goals. I wanted to settle in, make friends, find work and get pregnant. But I got more specific. These were my goals for my first year in Germany:

1. Learn German
2. Develop a social network
3. Get my Coaching Diploma
4. Set up my business
5. Get pregnant

At the end of the first year, I went home for Christmas. I was living in Munich, had a group of friends, had created my Happiness Club, could speak some basic German, had become a Certified Life Coach and was 4 months pregnant.

And people said 'You are so lucky' over and over again. And I was like, NO. It wasn't luck, it was living with intention. Being lucky would imply that it was something external to me responsible for my success. I was proactive and clear on what I needed to do. I didn't just have vague goals of 'settling into Munich'.

- I immediately signed up for intensive German classes and completed 6 months of full time studying.
- I studied and gained my Certificate in Life Coaching.
- I set up my business ready to launch in January 2015.
- I actively changed my nutrition, exercise and supplements and sought support from an acupuncturist specialising in fertility.
- I pushed myself out of my comfort zone every day to go to events and created a social network independent of my partner.

I was clear on the life I wished to lead. I had clear specific goals. I actively worked towards them every day. I reviewed and revised what I wanted and needed to do. I was proactive and in control of my life.

Let me give you another current example. My health and nutrition journey. Last year I was really suffering. I had really bad hay fever. It was so bad that I had to get an inhaler to breathe and a steroid cream for my inflamed skin. My eyes itched so much that I felt tired as I peered out of my bloodshot eyes. It was really affecting my physical and mental energy. Added to that I was showing the first signs of perimenopausal symptoms. I felt very hormonal. Again this was affecting my life. And with a 4 year old son to run after, I knew I could not, and more importantly did not, want to continue this way. I sought out a wonderful nutritionist, Anna, who helped me understand what was going on in my body. With her guidance, I began to consciously and intentionally work on my diet. I didn't just say I want to be healthier. I didn't think I'd merely cut out a few things from my diet. Every single day for 6 weeks I followed an elimination diet and wow, what a difference. In 7 days my skin had cleared up and I didn't need an inhaler. After 4 weeks my skin and hair looked healthy and glowing. I lost a little weight and had so much more physical energy and mental clarity. And I felt hormonally balanced. I felt amazing. I now continue on the journey exploring deeper what is going on in my body and follow a healthy diet. This way I am consciously working on my health every day.

Does this resonate with you? I regularly listen to clients who tell me routinely things such as 'oh I love going to the Christmas markets but I probably won't make it again this year'. Or 'I really enjoy going to museums but I never go'. Or 'I enjoy being in the mountains but can never be bothered to do something on the weekends'. Sometimes we are so busy, we don't prioritise or place value on the things that bring us joy.

I love live music. Loud rock music. Nothing makes me happier than seeing my favourite bands live. And it creates long-lasting happy memories for me. For a long time after I moved to Munich, I didn't know where the venues were. I didn't know anyone who liked the same music and I also had a young child. But I realised that I was doing the same as my clients. Making excuses and not being intentional. So I started to go to gigs. By myself. And I can't tell you how happy it makes me! I now consciously choose to spend my precious time and money on going to concerts.

Wendy is a good friend and a great example of living an Intentional Life. For years she worked in a stressful and unsupportive environment. It was made worse by having to work shifts, which was taking its toll on her health. She reached a point where she felt she couldn't continue this way but felt very stuck and unsure of how to find something else. She was thinking about other possible jobs, all of which were in a similar vein and organisational structure. So I asked her: 'If you could do anything for a living, what would you do?'. Her face lit up and she replied that she had always wanted to be a writer. So we explored how she could begin to do something with that to initially help counterbalance the negativity of her current work. The upshot was that she combined two passions, writing and travel, to create a travel blog. Wendy then worked on getting much more clarity on the life she wished to lead and becoming proactive in her goals to make them happen. Fast forward a couple of years and Wendy has bought a home with a garden, quit her job, set up a successful dog walking business, a VA business and trained as a Pet Bereavement Counsellor. She adopted a beautiful dog and has just written her first book. Wow! It's a long way from the stressed out and the constantly sick woman she was just a couple of years before. This is the power of living intentionally and proactively.

Emily is another great example of Intentional Happiness. She came to me wanting to make significant changes in her life. She had big dreams but was feeling overwhelmed with day to day life and was struggling to create a routine and find space to work on her career goals. We worked together to initially carve out a morning routine and to schedule in regular commitments. She identified tasks that could be delegated and found a babysitter for her young son for a few hours per week. She developed a routine and found space to focus on her long term goals. Together we got clarity on what she wanted to work on and once she got that clarity she ran with it. She is an amazing example of being proactive in her life. Emily is now the highly successful founder of Dating To Get Married teaching people the skills to create soulmate love.

This is what Intentional Happiness is!

ONE LAST THING BEFORE WE START

I'm only human. I don't get it right every day. Many days I'm fully focused and completely intentional. Sometimes I manage half of it. Sometimes a few days go by and I catch myself getting caught up in the busyness of life. I then acknowledge this and try to talk to myself with compassion and refocus. What I'm saying is, do your best. Be conscious of your actions, of your attention slipping and realign again. But don't beat yourself up if you skip days. It's normal. You are human. Life gets busy. Don't put pressure on yourself. Simply move forwards proactively in your life, keep doing your best to be intentional.

I'm now going to take you step-by-step on the Intentional Happiness Journey. Take your time and complete each chapter before moving on. As a guide, in the Intentional Happiness Circle we complete one step per month. It will pay dividends to spend time now getting these foundations in place.

Enjoy the journey!

PART 2

CHAPTER 5

VISUALIZE YOUR FUTURE SELF

To begin your journey towards Intentional Happiness, the starting point has to be working out exactly what your Happy Life looks like. Hopefully, you have already taken the Happiness Quiz and have a baseline on your happiness. Now you can get a clearer picture of what you want to reach for. One of the best ways to do this is to visualize your future self.

Visualization is a powerful tool for gaining clarity on exactly what you want and living an Intentional Life. When you are clear on where you want to go and what the life you wish to lead looks like, you will be more prepared to take the steps needed to get there.

In Shelley Taylor's research, her studies show that visualization can help with problem-solving, goal attainment and health behaviour change. Focusing on the process during the visualization, rather than the goal, reduces stress and brings goal attainment.

There are also studies that link mental imagery with neuroscience. Stephen Kosslyn is a pioneer in this field and has shown how the brain sees little difference between reality and mental imagery. So visualizing positive outcomes and life goals helps create a positive mindset and enhance the Law of Attraction.

Most of the time, many people are so busy rushing through life or trying to look busy and interesting on Facebook, that they don't stop to ask themselves what it is they really want. Some people don't believe they can have the things they desire. Or are too scared to stop and dig deep. And many people I work with feel they should be happy because they have the job, car, house, family, money, etc.

Having a positive mindset is so important. Believing that you can have this life you desire is an essential part of visualizing and then creating that life. This quote from Henry Ford, '*Whether you think you can or whether you think you can't, you're right*' sums it up well. Believing things are possible is crucial to having the life you desire.

No one thought you could run a mile in under 4 minutes until Roger Bannister did it in 1954. Now that record has been smashed several times. In 2004 John Reese became the first person to earn $1million in 1 day. Before that, no one believed that was possible. After John Reese did it, many have also achieved this success. And in my years of experience, the lives that people wish for are almost always realistic and attainable.

So let's take some time now to begin to gain some clarity.

EXERCISE 1: FUTURE SELF VISUALIZATION

I'd like to take you through a guided visualization. You can download my Future Self Visualization here. It will help you gain clarity on the life you wish to lead. Find some uninterrupted time (around 30 minutes) and a quiet space. Grab a pen and paper and listen to the visualization. Afterwards, spend some time writing down what you visualized.

http://julieleonardcoaching.com/guided-future-visualization/

Alternatively, you can use the questions I use in the visualization script to guide you to find the answers.

Write down the answers to the following questions:

In what location would you like to live? What does it look like? Are you by the sea, in the mountains, in a city, in the countryside? Is it the place you are in right now? How does it look? How does it smell? How does it feel? Is it warm, sunny, cold? What noises can you hear? Where would you like to be?

What does your ideal home look like? What is it made of?

What colour is it? What size is it? Is it an apartment, a house? How many floors does it have? Take a walk around. How is it decorated, in what colours? How does your home feel? Is it calm? Is it noisy and busy? Who lives there? Are there special rooms? A nursery, a den, an office, a quiet room?

Who are you sharing your life with? Is there a husband, wife, partner, kids, animals, neighbours, friends, colleagues? Who is sharing this ideal life with you?

In this ideal home, in this ideal location, what do you look like? How do you feel? Are you healthy, do you feel strong? What are you wearing? What does your wardrobe look like? Can you feel how you feel right at this moment? Are you confident? Happy? Content? Calm? Peaceful?

What does your ideal body look like and feel like?

What are you doing for a living? What is your ideal job? What does that ideal job look like? How does it feel? What are you doing that gives you meaning and purpose in your life? Are you following your passion, are you following your heart?

What else are you doing in your life that brings you meaning and purpose? What are your hobbies? What are your activities you enjoy?

How do you feel on a daily basis? What is your state of mind?

What is the ideal amount of money in your bank account?

What are the 3 things you are grateful for right now?

You now have a clear vision of the life you wish to lead. And a foundation from which to work from.

EXERCISE 2: CONSIDER MAKING A VISION BOARD

I personally love to reinforce my vision by creating an Intentional Happiness Vision Board.

When you gain clarity and have focus on what you want and your conscious brain sees it every day, you become more aware of opportunities connected to your desires. Vision Boards add clarity to your desires. Simply put, a vision board is a visual representation of the things you wish to see. For example, you take a large piece of paper and some magazines and cut out images of the life you wish. Such as, if you want to live in Tokyo, so you choose a picture of Tokyo. Or you want a family, so you choose a picture of children. Or you can choose pictures that evoke a feeling. For example, a woman meditating that makes you feel calm and less stressed.

When you surround yourself with these images of who you want to become, what you want to have, where you live and who with, your life changes to match these desires. That is how powerful the mind is! (Remember the research on neuroscience.)

How does it work?

Have you ever set a New Years' resolution only for it not last past February? The reason is that we often make our goals too vague. I want to be healthy. I need to exercise. I want more money. I want a beautiful house….. The problem here is that these are just wishes, they have no real intention behind them. They are not specific enough.

With **intention** comes **clarity** and with clarity comes **change**.

We are bombarded on a daily basis with images and information which our brains have to filter. Has this ever happened to you? You are chatting to a friend who tells you she went to a movie last night and you hadn't even heard of it. Then after that conversation, you begin to see posters of the movie, read reviews and hear people talking about it. The reason for this is that we have blindspots. It's not that the information wasn't around, it's just that our brains weren't consciously looking for it.

And this takes us to The Law of Attraction. Let me give you an example to explain it. Say you want to change jobs. Like I said at the beginning, if you keep it vague it will get you nowhere. But if you have a clear idea of what exactly you want then it means your brain is now consciously filtering the information it receives. It's looking for ways to align all that information you are bombarded with, with what you want. Which is a new (specific) job.

When you know what you want, you actively seek out ways to get it. You are open to opportunities to make it happen and you consciously draw what you want to you.

Let's recap. Vision boards:

- Help us gain clarity on our goals.
- Create a positive mindset.
- Remove blindspots.

Another way I create beautiful vision boards is on my computer. When I'm clear on what my goals for Intentional Happiness are, I simply find the images and create gorgeous boards on my laptop. There are many collage programmes you can choose from such as Fotojet.com

Well done! You now have a much clearer idea of the life you are aiming for and what it is that makes you Intentionally Happy. The next step is to turn your dreams into goals.

CHAPTER 6

GOAL SETTING

Now that you have more clarity on what you want in your life and how it should look, it's time to set some goals to create your Intentional Life.

Why?

Because setting and achieving goals can transform your life!

Goals are the way we turn our dreams into reality. And research shows that setting and working towards goals can contribute to our happiness. By setting goals we focus our attention on what is important.

GOAL SETTING AND HAPPINESS

"Find a happy person, and you will find a project," writes Sonja Lyubomirsky. Her research has found that goal setting greatly affects our happiness levels. More specifically, it's the types of goals and the pursuit of those goals that are important. The simple act of creating goals and having a positive mindset already has a huge impact on our happiness.

When we're focusing on a goal, even our physical health is better. In an experiment, Flow researcher Mihaly Csikszentmihalyi messaged people throughout the day and asked them to report what they were doing and how they felt. They reported fewer physical symptoms when working on a goal – and more symptoms when alone, on the weekends, and with nothing to do.

Goal setting also has spillover effects into other areas of life. We increase our well-being when we make progress towards our goals (unsurprisingly), but we also increase life satisfaction in other unrelated areas of our life. For example, going to the gym more often could make us happier in our relationships.

Goals are so powerful because they make us feel hopeful and confident. They add a sense of structure and meaning to life, and we feel happy setting, working on and achieving them.

However, a 2018 study also highlighted that having goals is not quite enough to create happiness. In line with Sonja Lyubomirsky, the authors of this 2018 study refer to the research of Tim Kasser about Intrinsic Goals and Extrinsic Goals. People who pursue Intrinsic Goals (e.g. personal growth, relationships, community giving and health) are happier than those pursuing Extrinsic Goals (e.g. wealth, fame, etc.). Of course, some extrinsic goals are important and necessary, but be sure to have more intrinsic goals than extrinsic goals for a happier and more fulfilling life.

The famous study (mentioned in chapter 1) about income and life satisfaction, where emotional well-being peaks at about $75,000 and life satisfaction at $95,000 indicates that there is more to life than just earning money.

How people approach the goal is also something worth mentioning. People who have a goal to avoid something (Avoidance) are less happy than people who work towards something (Approach). The same goes for the idea of the outcome. People who are more focused on the Outcome or Performance of a goal, are less happy than people who focus on the Process of achieving a goal. Focusing on the process is what Mihaly Csikszentmihalyi considers getting into a flow state, which increases happiness.

The authors of the 2018 study concluded that there is mounting evidence that shifting to a process-based focus brings more happiness. This is also in line with what Carol Dweck coined as a growth mindset. As growth in itself is important in Dweck's theory, it also links back to Tim Kasser's research on intrinsic goals. As personal growth is an intrinsic goal, he found that it makes people happier.

To summarise:

- Pick 3-5 goals to work on.
- Focus on the process, not just the outcome. Adopt a growth mindset.
- Create a positive mindset that you can achieve your goals.
- Have more intrinsic than extrinsic goals.
- Actively work towards something (Approach).

There are many personal barriers to change such as lack of motivation, lack of energy, lack of desire, fear of change or of the unknown, fear of failure, lack of focus, feeling lost, not knowing what we want. They all keep us stuck and unable to move on. (If you are finding that you feel stuck due to negative thoughts and limiting beliefs then please reach out to me, or another coach for help. Coaches like myself can get you unstuck and on the path to the life you want very quickly.)

But right now, here is a tip for you. One that I use all the time myself and with my clients. It really helps shift your focus in a more positive way.

Focus on your **WHY**.

So I know that I want to be healthy and to do so I need to exercise. Here's the thing. I don't enjoy exercising. And I haven't found much exercise I enjoy. I can easily lose momentum and consistency in my exercising. Because if I focus on the What, it really isn't that attractive. Hit the gym? I'd rather curl up with a book. But if I focus on my Why, then I find my motivation. I want to be healthy. I want to have the energy to run after my young son. I want to feel strong. I want to feel sexy. I want to enjoy cake and wine and still fit in my skinny jeans.

Find your why and you will find your motivation.

In my experience, one of the biggest reasons people don't reach their goals is that they make them too vague. Typically we say things like: I want to lose weight. I want to eat healthily. I want to get fit. I want a new job. I want to find love. These are the ultimate goals, but there is no real plan of action. If there is no plan then we often give up quickly. And if you want to create a new habit, research tells us that it takes at least 21 days to make something a habit, longer if it's something big.

Here are my 10 tips to achieving your goals:

1. Identify your goal – big or small.
2. Write it down – writing down our goals increases our chances of sticking to them.

3. Be specific – e.g. how much weight do you want to lose, how exactly will you do it.

4. Accountability – tell someone your plans and ask them to be your accountability partner.

5. Set goals – break your goal down into small steps and set achievable sub-goals.

6. Plan your first step – getting started can be the hardest part.

7. Reflect – make time to regularly check-in and see how far you have come. It keeps the momentum going.

8. Ask for help – get the right support, advice and motivation from a professional. There are excellent Personal Trainers, Life Coaches and Nutritionists all trained to support you to reach your goals.

9. Tackle one goal at a time – trying to change everything at once is less likely to work.

10. Celebrate – when you reach your goal take time to celebrate all that you have achieved. Think about what you enjoyed and learned along the way. Then, set the next one!

Ok, let's get goal planning!

We are going to use the SMART method of goal setting - Specific, Measurable, Achievable, Result-Based, Timed.

In their book A Theory of Goal Setting and Task Performance, Edwin A. Locke and Gary P. Latham found through their research that a goal is more attainable if it's specific and challenging (but achievable). They also outline five other characteristics for successful goal setting. The goal needs to be:

1. Clear (specific).
2. Challenging (but achievable).
3. Entered with a sense of commitment.
4. Invite feedback.
5. Consider the complexity of the task and create sub-goals.

Locke's early research inspired Dr. G. Doran to develop the acronym for SMART goals.

So, let's be goal getters!

Ideally, pick a maximum of 3-5 goals. Use this table as a template to break down your goal and see how you will achieve it. Use separate tables for each goal.

GOAL	
SPECIFIC	
MEASURABLE	
ACHIEVABLE	
RESULT	
TIMED	

Example

GOAL	I want to feel fitter
SPECIFIC	Yoga twice per week Couch-to-5K training
MEASURABLE	Increase in stamina Increase in mood Increased flexibility Increased running distance
ACHIEVABLE	Immediately start yoga twice per week. Begin Couch-to-5k, 9-week programme, 30 minutes 3 times per week
RESULT	Yoga twice per week Can run 5k
TIMED	9-week programme, 30 minutes each time Yoga, 1 hour x 2 per week Results in 2 months.

You now have clear specific goals to intentionally work on.

CHAPTER 7

KNOW YOUR VALUES

Values are an integral part of who we are. They are a unique part of our personality.

Often when we are not living in alignment with our core values we can feel unsettled and unhappy with inner turmoil.

When we become conscious of our values we can live more intentionally in alignment with them. And feel happy, content and peaceful.

In his Goal-Setting Theory, Locke also mentions that setting goals aligned with your values make them more achievable.

Values affect our thinking and behaviour. So if an important value is to be healthy then we modify our behaviour to be more healthy.

Most of us don't know our values. It's hard to sit ourselves down and dig deep enough to know what we truly value, rather than think of values we *should* have.

So, I suggest you sit with a Coach or block off an hour of time to follow these exercises.

Let's get started.

EXERCISE 1

Please note: It's better to work through the exercises rather than select values from a list. When we select from a list, we can have a tendency to choose values that seem better, but may not honestly be who we are. But if you need inspiration then an online search will give you some lists.

1. Write down all the values you have that immediately come to mind. There is no limit on how many values you list.

2. Next, ask yourself some questions to dig deeper.

    *   Think of an important experience or moment in your life. What happened? How did you feel? What values were strong in that moment? Write them down.

    *   Think of a negative experience that made you upset, angry, frustrated. What happened? How did it make you feel? What value(s) were you suppressing? Write them down.

    *   What is most important in your life in order for you to feel happy and fulfilled? For instance,

53

health, surrounded by nature, travel, continual learning, etc. What values must you follow to feel this and not feel incomplete?

- What values are essential to your life?
- What are the most important values to support your inner self?

3. Now take this whole list of values and group them into themes. e.g. learning, growth and personal development. Or connection, intimacy, belonging, relationships.

4. Now select a word that sums up each category. We are looking for an optimum 5-10 values. Looking at them, how do they make you feel? Are they in alignment with who you are? Are they personal to you? Are there any that don't sit right with you? Adjust your list if you need to.

5. Now rank them in order of importance.

6. Create a memorable phrase for each one to give it more meaning and make it more powerful. E.g. Health: To nurture and nourish my body every day.

7. To ensure your values align with your intentional living, you could also create a table, similar to the one suggested by Scott Jeffrey. The score is how intentionally you are living this value.

8. Review this table monthly.

9. Use this table to support your goal setting and ensure you lead an Intentional Life.

Rank	Value	Score (0-10)	Action to Increase
1	Equality	8	Offer a free coaching place to a woman experiencing trauma
2	Kindness	9	Do one act of kindness a day
3	Honesty/ Authenticity	8	Embrace vulnerability
4	Learning/Growth	9	Read 2 self development or non-fiction books per month
5	Taking responsibility	7	Work on my exercise goals daily and take responsibility!

CHAPTER 8

TIME MANAGEMENT

As we begin to move forward to create and achieve the life you desire, I want to share with you some time management tools. I have found them simple yet highly effective in planning and achieving what I want in life.

Research on students who improved their time management skills showed a positive effect on their perceived performance and life satisfaction. If you want to be happy and focused on your goals then learning to manage and prioritise your time for what is important is essential.

Here are my 6 steps to freeing up time and creating space to prioritise your happiness:

1. 168 HOURS

There are not enough hours in the day! I hear this a lot and I've uttered it many times myself in the past. Do you feel constantly busy? Are you on the go from morning till night? At the end of the day, do you collapse on the couch in an exhausted heap? Do all your good intentions of the day go out the window and instead of a healthy snack or tackling a project, you zone out on Netflix and wine?

In our busy lifestyles where we are rewarded for looking and being busy, it's easy to feel overwhelmed and exhausted. And when we try to set goals or make changes we often end up trying to squeeze things into our already overfilled schedules. This cannot work long term. I know this from a few years ago when I wanted to start exercising. I had an extremely busy job. Most days I worked overtime and each day I was mentally exhausted. I kept trying to fit in some exercise but often it was too late, or I needed to eat or I felt too tired or unmotivated. If I did find some time it was completely inconsistent and unsustainable.

Breaking a day down and thinking of it as 24 hours helps us to see it as a wider stretch of time. But what I have found even more helpful in terms of seeing just how much time we have in our lives is to think of our time over 1 week. Or 168 hours. When we start to think of 168 hours instead of just 24 hours we begin to see how possible it's to do things we really want to do. The things that will make and sustain our happiness. So, let's get started!

EXERCISE 1: Time Tracker

For one week, keep a record of how you spend each day. Break each day down into 30 minute sections. Record everything! Breakfast, getting ready, work, errands, Facebook, social media, emails, television, lunch, dinner, sleep. Absolutely everything you do in a day, every day for 7 days.

After 7 days, take some time to sit down and look at what you have been doing. Any surprises? Be honest, is there a lot of time on social media? Time that could be used more productively? Things that aren't taking you forwards in your goals and living with more intention? Unproductive time? Mark areas with potential for change.

2. Diarize

The next step is to take your calendar and put in all the non-negotiable appointments and commitments you have each week.

EXERCISE 2

Take a blank calendar and put in your fixed appointments. The things that must be done. This includes work, taking kids to school/childcare and picking them up, healthcare appointments, courses and classes, after-school activities, meals and sleep. Once that is done, you should now see clear blocks of time available where you can start to do things that make you happy.

3. Write a Not-To-Do List

I love writing lists and always have a daily to-do list. For a long time it felt that I had an endless to-do list and was always so busy and not always achieving the big projects. Then I watched a talk by Dan Sullivan and it really resonated with me. He shared a great tool to help you identify activities in your life that you don't have to do yourself. This exercise can be applied to work as well as your personal life. I initially used it to manage my business but I have found it highly effective when applied to my personal life too.

EXERCISE 3

Take some paper and a pen and create 3 columns. Give column 1 the title Dislike. This is where you list all the things you hate doing, column 2 has the title Like and is for all the things you like doing and column 3 has the heading Love and is for things you love doing.

Think of your life right now and look at the list of all the things you collated in Exercise 1. Now take some time to put them ALL into either column 1, 2 or 3.

1.DISLIKE	2. LIKE	3.LOVE
grocery shopping	*reading*	*yoga classes*
doing my taxes	*studying courses*	*playing with my son*

4. Delegate

From your list of all the things you dislike, are there things that you can delegate? Are there other people you can delegate to? E.g. cleaner, babysitter, have shopping delivered, finances? Things that you don't actually need to do?

EXERCISE 4

Make a list of tasks that could be delegated and begin the process of removing them, delegating to other family members or outsourcing.

5. Learn to say NO

Do YOU have to do all of it? Can chores be divided amongst family members? Are there commitments you can withdraw from that no longer interest you or serve your happiness. That no longer fits with the Intentional Life you envisage? Are you spending time with people who don't lift you up and make you feel amazing? Or doing things out of duty or loyalty that doesn't bring you joy?

EXERCISE 5

From your list above, what can you say No to now? Write them down. Begin to work down the list removing things in your life that aren't serving your purpose or that *you* don't need to do. Some examples of things I removed or delegated are:

> Paying someone to do my taxes.
> Left a moms group that I had outgrown.
> Unsubscribed to newsletters I never read.
> Removed Facebook 'friends' I had never met.
> Removed Facebook friends I am no longer friends with.
> Left in-person and online groups that I am no longer interested in.

6. Block off time

Now let's begin to plan in your goals and what you need to do to work intentionally towards them.

EXERCISE 6

Revisit your goals. Review the space in your 168 hours per week and schedule in time for the activities you wish to explore. I highly recommend blocking off time in your calendar. E.g. for exercise, learning a language, hiking, reading, etc. Remember to schedule in regular breaks.

In those blocks of time, work on one project at a time. Ever feel like you have run around all day and not got anything done? Worked all day on your laptop but never got that report finished. Are you jumping between tasks? Multitasking? One of the more effective tools you can employ is to work on one project at a time. Don't go on to the next thing until you complete it. If you are writing a report, focus on that until it's complete. Don't check emails and get sidetracked. Not only will you have a sense of accomplishment, but you will also get far more done.

When you are blocking off time for your goals, think about placing them on your Optimal Productivity Time. For example, I am at my most creative between 11-3. So that is when I create content for my business or see my coaching clients. I also work well late at night and in silence. So when I'm writing my books I do this around 8-11 at night. I then schedule easier tasks like emails first thing in the morning or in the evening. Think about your tasks and your energy and how to pace out your day and your week.

A useful technique to help get into the flow, instill a sense of urgency and set realistic time blocks is the Pomodoro Technique. The Pomodoro Technique is a time management method developed by Francesco Cirillo in the 1980s. The technique uses a timer to break down work into intervals, usually 25 minutes in length, separated by 5 minute breaks. Each interval is known as a *pomodoro*, from the Italian word for 'tomato'. It's named after the tomato-shaped kitchen timer that Cirillo used as a university student.

Sometimes we can be less productive when we feel we have all day. I know I work better because I actually have fewer hours during the day to work. With a young son who is in daycare until 2 pm each day, I have to get my work done in just a few hours. That makes me work smarter not harder. And breaking work or other goals into 25 minute blocks helps me keep my focus entirely on the project in hand.

CHAPTER 9

DECLUTTERING

Now, let's explore how to create even more time and space to focus on your goals. Imagine what you could do with more time. More time to focus on the important things in your life.

How much time are you wasting looking for an outfit, lost keys or a piece of paperwork? How many minutes do you lose per day, per month, per year? What is the impact on your health, stress levels and happiness? How could you better use that time?

Let me ask you:

Do you often feel harassed and out of control whilst looking for something?

Do you avoid dealing with the issue until you are confronted by it? E.g. you can't find an important piece of paperwork, or a clean top, or you realise your passport needs to be renewed right before your holiday?

Does finding something become a time consuming process?

Do you spend time hunting for something without success?

Do you look around at all you need to sort and then feel too tired to tackle it? Or feel overwhelmed about where to start?

Does clutter feel like noise to you that blocks your creativity and motivation?

Clutter has an effect on you both physically and emotionally. Things physically take up space in your home and can affect your health. And clutter can leave you drained and lacking in energy and motivation, with low levels of concentration and feeling more emotional and overwhelmed.

When I worked in Glasgow and spent time in people's homes, I could see the direct impact of clutter on their lives. I could also see that when I supported them with the psychological root of the clutter, as well as rolling up my sleeves and helping them get organized, how adversely it affected them. And how their emotional and physical health improved once we had tackled it. Here's what I saw.

The Negative Impact of Clutter:

    Stress
    Anxiety
    Depression

Feeling Overwhelmed

Feeling Worried

Being Tearful

Lack of concentration

No focus

Little time

No headspace

Reduced creativity

Reduced motivation

Depleted energy

Quite a list isn't it! Did you realise how much of a real impact clutter can have on your life? It should not be underestimated. It's not simply about having less stuff or being tidy. It's about a real change of mindset. To create a home and lifestyle that frees up time, space and energy to focus on and design a life that brings you joy and happiness.

Positive Impact of Decluttering:

Less Stress

Less Anxiety

Improved mood

Feeling in control

Feeling organised

More concentration

More clarity

More focus

More energy

More motivation

More time

Emotional balance

Calm

Relaxed

JOY

HAPPINESS

A life you desire

We live in a society where the media bombards us with images of what we are told we need to own in order to be happy. So many of our homes are full of stuff. There are many reasons why things often start to pile up and begin to feel out of control. The good news is that you can regain control. And remain decluttered and organised.

What's your level of tidy? Let me be clear, I'm not telling you how your home should look. Yes, I believe you need less stuff. That your home should be a reflection of you and your lifestyle. That it should feel homely and have items that bring you joy and happiness and/or are functional. If you feel calmer and happier if your home is more minimalist, with no 'noise' from clutter, then that is what you aim for. If you like having lots of knick-knacks and pictures and other things in your home then declutter to that level. Declutter to your personal level of what you feel is homely.

And just before we start decluttering, let's talk about the reasons for your clutter. Over my many years of supporting people to get organised I have observed many reasons for the build up of clutter:

Busy Lives
Too much stuff
Media, society
Low mood / emotional health
Feeling overwhelmed
Not sure where to start
Little or no storage solutions
Don't know where to donate
Guilt
Lack of time

Avoidance: Be honest with yourself. What are you avoiding dealing with?

Clearing clutter frees up more time to focus on what is important to us. What brings us joy and supports us in living an Intentional Life. This includes not only physical clutter but extends to digital and social media, relationships and commitments.

EXERCISE

Let's get started! Now decide which room you wish to start with. Rooms with less sentimental objects are easier to declutter first and will give you the motivation to continue. Unless there is something urgent then start with the small easy tasks that you can tick off and accomplish quickly. This will allow you to see the impact of what you are doing, give you a sense of achievement and increase your motivation. Sometimes the bigger tasks may have an emotional issue underlying it that will require work with your life coach to resolve.

Marie Kondo lists these categories in order of ease: Clothes, books, paperwork, Komono (all other things), Sentimental items. This can be a good place to start.

Over the years I have developed ten questions to help you declutter. If you are struggling to let go of something, hold it in your hand and ask yourself these questions.

1. Do I love it?
2. Do I need it?
3. Is it useful or beautiful?
4. Did I choose to bring it into my life?
5. Would it be hard to replace if I needed it again?
6. Does it hold meaning or have sentimental value?
7. Do I need to save it for tax or legal reasons?

8. If I were free from guilt would I still keep it?

9. Have I used it in the past year? Past 3 years? Past 5 years?

10. Does it fit with the vision of the life I wish to lead?

What do you need to declutter?

- Bin bags
- 4 sheets of paper that say KEEP, DONATE, RECYCLE, SELL.
- Cleaning products

Here is an example. If you decide to declutter your clothes first:

Step 1: Gather all your clothes together in your bedroom. Collect clothes, jackets and accessories from other rooms. Take everything out of your wardrobe.

Step 2: Place the 4 sheets of paper around your room. Take each piece in turn, decide which pile it goes on. Damaged, stained or extremely worn clothes can be binned or recycled. Then sort the rest into piles to keep, sell or donate. Ask yourself honestly: Do I love it? Does it bring me joy? Is it functional? Does it fit? And the big one: Does it make me feel fabulous? If you don't like something, don't keep it because it was expensive, or it was a gift or you might fit into it one day. Clear them out and only have a wardrobe of clothes that you love and makes you feel fabulous. I promise you, having fewer clothes, but the right clothes will give you many more outfit choices.

Step 3: Finish sorting through your clothes.

Step 4: Clean your wardrobe and drawers.

Step 5: Put back the clothes to keep.

Step 6: Take rubbish to the bin.

Step 7: Plan a date to take donations to charity/give to friends.

Follow this guide for books, toys, kitchen equipment and other categories.

Tidy For Function

I love Sheila Chandra's 'The Toothbrush Method'. Ever noticed that no matter how messy and disorganised you are, you can always find your toothbrush? It's right where you need it to be and you always return it to its place. Same with your shower gel and shampoo. You don't trail out of the shower and go look around the house for it. It's right where it needs to be in your shower. Apply the same principle around your house. Organise your belongings so they are where you use them.

Do I have to do it all at once? NO. But you will be amazed at what you can achieve in a few short hours. Organising your clothes may seem a huge task but you can manage it in 2-3 hours. Then that huge task is complete and you will feel satisfied that you finished the job. And you can tick it off your list.

But if that feels too overwhelming or you really can't spare huge chunks of time to tackle your clutter, then break it down into small manageable goals that take 10, 15, 30 minutes. Using the clothes example, clear one drawer at a time, or one subcategory at a time. E.g. socks, bras, jeans, gloves. A little each day soon adds up to a tidy and organised house.

Extra tip: Declutter first then buy storage. That way you buy exactly what you need.

And I promise you, decluttering and organising your home will free up time and headspace to focus on living your Intentionally Happy life.

CHAPTER 10

PROCRASTINATION

For around one year (yes, that long!) I procrastinated on something that needed to be done. As a UK citizen and with Brexit looming I wanted to convert my UK driving license to a German one. Currently, as a European Citizen, it's a straightforward project. But for months I put it off.

Initially, I had no idea how to go about it. I kept researching. With my limited German I felt deskilled in simply picking up the phone as I would have in the UK. Then I got a letter to say that Brexit may happen in April of that year and I knew I was on limited time. I got the answers, the documents and an appointment.

I was so nervous. It doesn't seem logical but anything bureaucratic makes me nervous. Combined with worrying that I can't communicate well in German lowered my confidence. As it was, I went to the appointment, it was completed in 10 minutes and I walked out of the building with a German license. Why did I not deal with it sooner?

Procrastination! And it annoys me that I can be like this. But I'm working on it and here I share some ways to tackle procrastination.

How is Procrastination related to Intentional Living?

First of all, people who procrastinate report lower levels of happiness. Secondly, procrastination is the opposite of Intention. Avoiding or delaying projects will not serve you well. It's one of the blocks which prevents you from achieving your goals and living intentionally.

What is Procrastination?

- Procrastination is not taking action.
- It's avoiding starting something you need or want to start.
- It's avoiding finishing something you're supposed to finish. Or never finishing projects you've started.
- It's doing something else, or sometimes absolutely anything else (hello laundry!), when you know you should be working on a specific project or meeting a deadline.

Researchers categorise procrastination into two types:

Decisional (putting off taking decisions) and
Avoidant (putting off doing things).

All of us procrastinate sometimes. But some of us do it more often than others or in certain areas of our lives.

There are many reasons for procrastination:

- Uninteresting work
- Lack of confidence in ability
- Anxiety
- Perfectionism
- Lack of time management skills
- Fear

And the impact of procrastination is high:

- Stress!
- Lower levels of happiness
- Missing deadlines
- Missing opportunities
- Financial or reputation costs
- Not living intentionally
- Not reaching goals

Habits of non-procrastinators

By looking at the habits of people who don't procrastinate we can get an idea of how to deal with it. Here are some tools to support you overcome your procrastination.

1. Block out periods of time to work on a specific piece of work. Work only on that until it's completed or the time is finished. (Remember our chapter on time management and the Pomodoro Technique.)

2. Tackle the big stuff first. Get the issue out of the way and you will feel better. (Like the relief I felt when I got my license and could have saved myself all that stress).

3. Dig deep to understand the why of your procrastination (what's really behind your procrastination?).

4. Have no zero days (do something every day towards your goals - see chapter 11).

5. Don't leave things until the last minute (and then get in a panic or feel mega stressed).

6. Have clarity on your goals and break them down into manageable steps that you regularly review. (Hey, you're already doing that!)

7. Adopt a Growth Mindset. Recognise that you can keep building and developing your skills and personal growth.

The following exercises will help you challenge your procrastination. Grab a pen and paper and let's do this!

EXERCISE 1

What areas of your life do you procrastinate in? Identify and write them down.

EXERCISE 2

Dig deep. Why are you procrastinating here? Really. Is it fear? Anxiety? Low self worth? Lack of Time management? What holds you back? Write it down.

EXERCISE 3

7 Day Procrastination Challenge

Choose one thing off your list. Is there something in your life that you need to tackle and you're avoiding or putting off dealing with? Or something you want to work on connected to your Intentional Happiness that you need to focus on? Set yourself a goal of tackling and completing it in the next 7 days. Choose a small, manageable one. And remember for added motivation, focus on your Why. At the end of 7 days, you will be one step closer to your Intentionally Happy Life.

CHAPTER 11

NO ZERO DAYS

We have all had those days. You have lots of goals you want to achieve. Good intentions to do that workout, eat a healthy lunch, do some work, read a book... And before you know it, it's bedtime and you didn't do anything you hoped to do.

Then sometimes several days go by and you don't achieve anything towards your goal. It's so easy then to be disheartened or to give up, thinking what's the point?

Well, let me introduce you to the concept of **No Zero Days**. A simple yet highly effective idea that will keep you motivated and focused on your goals.

The concept was first coined by a Reddit user when he commented on a post:

> 'Didn't' do anything all fucking day and it's 11:58 PM? Write one sentence. One push up. Read one page of that chapter. One. Because one is non zero'.

The way to keep focused, to continually move forward with your goals and to maintain living intentionally, is to do something every day. No matter how small it is towards that goal. To *never* have a Zero Day.

EXERCISE

So think of your goals you have set for this year. What is the minimum you can do each day to ensure that you're always making progress? Take that list of goals and write down beside each one, what the minimum is you can do each day to work towards that goal.

Remember to be intentional. E.g. exercising might mean taking a 15 minute walk every day. Or writing a book might mean writing for 10 minutes per day. Or reading a book. Reading one paragraph is better than reading nothing. And so on. Each day, look at your list of goals and do something, no matter how small it is towards that goal.

What you will find over time, is that you won't just do the minimum each day. It has a snowball effect and you will gradually increase what you do as you gather momentum and motivation.

CHAPTER 12

MOVING OUT OF YOUR COMFORT ZONE

In order to progress towards the life you wish to Intentionally lead, it's inevitable that you will need to, at various points on your journey, push yourself out of your comfort zone.

Fear regularly prevents us from taking that step out of our comfort zone. It's much less scary to stay where we are. But if we want to change, change doesn't happen in our comfort zone.

So think about what your goals are and what you may need to confront in order to move forward with your goals. What do you need to change in yourself to become the person you wish to be and to lead the life you intentionally want?

From a positive psychology perspective, staying too long in the Comfort Zone, means that the hedonic adaptation takes over. Sonja Lyubomirsky writes that people very quickly get used to both positive and negative experiences. You constantly have to create activities to stay happy. Therefore, you could argue that staying in your comfort zone makes you less happy.

This is also in line with what Mihaly Csikszentmihalyi writes in his book 'Flow'. He believes that 'flow' lies in the area between boredom and anxiety. But in order to stay in the flow, you will constantly need to challenge yourself. This is because you learn and grow accustomed to the new situation. So, we need to continue to expand our comfort zone.

Locke's goal-setting theory also supports this. He states that the goal needs to be challenging, but not too challenging, to achieve best results. A goal should be broken down into sub-goals and tasks to avoid overwhelm. This is a method to slowly step outside your comfort zone

We know that fear is what is keeping us in the comfort zone. Brené Brown's research into vulnerability breaks this down further. She shows that it's fear of being seen as vulnerable that stops us from stepping out of our comfort zone. To overcome this, we have to learn how to be vulnerable.

Here are some ideas on how to move out of your comfort zone:

1. **Disconnect from tech**. Facebook and Instagram often leave us comparing ourselves to others and

feeling negative about ourselves. This can keep us in our comfort zone if we feel we don't measure up to others. Stop comparing yourself to others by limiting your screen time.

2. **Find a role model who inspires you.** Is there someone famous you admire? Someone you know that leads their life in a way you wish to emulate? What do they do to be the person that you admire?

3. **Surround yourself with people who are positive and uplifting, who make you feel awesome.** It's pretty simple. Being around people that make you feel great and who believe in you means you have the support and encouragement when you move out of your comfort zone.

4. **Take small incremental steps to reach your goal.** Break it down into small, manageable steps that will take you forwards.

5. **Try something new until it feels comfortable.** Many things in life take practice. From the day you were born you have been learning and practicing and growing. Pick something you want to do and keep practicing until it feels comfortable.

6. **Agree to something you wouldn't normally do.** This is the most straightforward way to get out of your comfort zone. Try something new!

7. **Keep a list of Growth Goals.** I personally love this one. We usually keep a to-do list of practical things that need doing. But do you have a growth goals list? A list of personal development goals you work on and consciously keep in the forefront of your mind? These could include; adopting a growth mindset, embracing failure, learning to forgive, practice mindfulness or be more vulnerable.

8. **Join Toastmasters.** Many members of my groups already do this. They tell me that they have gained so much from it, especially increased confidence and getting out of their comfort zone.

What else would you add to this list?

EXERCISE

Thinking about your goals:

- What, if anything, has held you back from achieving them?
- What small next steps can you map out to move out of your comfort zone and closer to the Intentional Life you desire?

If I'm honest, I actually prefer to talk about expanding my comfort zone as opposed to stepping out of it. It's more positive and in alignment with a growth mindset and doesn't sound as scary! As you get clear on what you want, take small, measurable steps towards your goals and grow in confidence.

CHAPTER 13

FINDING BALANCE

As we reach the final few steps of living Intentionally, the topic of finding balance is timely. It draws together many of the topics we have already begun to reflect on and practice.

Leading an Intentional life means leading a balanced life. Ensuring that you spend time on and prioritise all areas of your life without neglecting any one area. Being intentional with both the Internal (mind, heart and health) and External (work, family, social).

Finding balance is always going to be an ongoing process. It requires us to prioritize our time as well as what's important to us. We need to set goals and be specific in what we want and need.

Relevant previous topics to review and reflect on here are:

- Goals
- Values

- Time management
- No zero days

How do we create balance in our lives?

Here are 10 ways:

1. **Boundaries.** Setting boundaries supports us to maintain healthy relationships and healthy lives. In order to do so, we need to understand our limits.

Exercise:

- Take some time to write down the answer to this question: What are your physical and emotional limits?
- Tune in to your feelings. You know, that feeling in your stomach when you feel uncomfortable, stressed or feeling resentful. When you know it's the wrong decision.
- Be assertive. If someone steps over your boundaries, learn to say NO!

2. **JOMO.** This is one of my favourites! JOMO (Joy Of Missing Out). So often we have FOMO (Fear Of Missing Out) but I actually love reclaiming JOMO. And embracing the joy that comes from respecting your boundaries, your values, your time or your needs. Sometimes you need to say

no without fear that you are missing out on something and enjoy doing the right thing for you.

3. **Revisit your values and goals.** Often we feel out of balance if we are not living in alignment with our values. Take time to revisit your values from chapter 7. Being conscious of your values will help you make decisions on what you do and who you do it with. The same is true for knowing your goals and being specific in the life you want. With everything you do, ask yourself: Is this in alignment with my values and goals?

4. **Be fully present.** A significant part of Living Intentionally and feeling balanced, especially internally, is to be fully present in all that you do, as often as possible.

5. **Self-care.** In order to have balance in our lives, it's essential to prioritise and acknowledge the importance of making time for 'Me Time'. What is your self-care routine? What works for you? Is it consistent? Is it daily? Are you making it a priority?

6. **Be intentional in all areas of your life.** Obviously! It's the whole point of the book! Friends, family, work, fun, spiritual. Take time to reflect on each area of your life. Are you being intentional in each aspect? What is important to you? What do you do every day to ensure you are being intentional?

7. **Prioritise what's important and your time!** You know

your values, you have identified your goals, you have visualised the life you wish to lead. Now make the time and prioritise all that is important.

8. **Nurture your network**. We are naturally social creatures. Connection and relationships are integral to our happiness and living with Intention, but it's often something that slips when we are too busy. Declutter toxic relationships, surround yourself with the right people who get you, love you, support you and inspire you. And then nurture and invest in that network.

9. **Have Fun.** Make sure you have fun and laughter in your life. Prioritise activities and hobbies that you love. That brings you joy, nurtures your health and your heart and deepens connections.

10. **Give Yourself Permission.** Let go of any guilt. Silence that inner critic. Say goodbye to limiting beliefs and give yourself permission to set boundaries. Say No! Go after the life you desire and live an Intentional Life.

EXERCISE

Which of the points on the list do you need to work on in order to feel more balance in your life? Write them down and next to them write down what actionable steps you can take right now.

CHAPTER 14

INTEGRITY

"Happiness is when what you think, what you say, and what you do are in harmony."

Mahatma Gandhi

Those of you who know me, know that I am a huge admirer of the work of Brené Brown. For those of you who don't know her, check out her TEDtalk on vulnerability (one of the top 5 most-watched TEDtalks) https://www.youtube.com/watch?v=iCvmsMzlF7o. In her latest book, Dare To Lead, she talks about integrity and it really resonated with me. How in order to lead a happy and Intentional Life we need to live with integrity.

As a research professor, she analysed all her data and created a powerful definition that captures the depth and importance of this concept:

'Integrity is choosing courage over comfort; it's choosing what's right over what's fun, fast or easy; and it's practising your values, not just professing them.'

Dare to Lead, Brené Brown 2018

Integrity is also a component of one of the Character Strengths from the VIA Institute, a non-profit personality research organisation. There are 24 Character strengths and integrity is an integral part of Honesty and is part of the virtue of 'Courage'. The VIA Institute claims that practicing these character strengths and virtues lead to greater well being.

The founders of the VIA Institute, Christopher Peterson and Martin E. P. Seligman, define Integrity within the strength of honesty as:

'When you are honest, you speak the truth. More broadly, you present yourself in a genuine and sincere way, without pretense, and taking responsibility for your feelings and actions. You are a person of integrity — you are who you say you are — and you act consistently across the domains of your life rather than being one way in the community and a completely different way in your family. As a result, you believe you are being consistently true to yourself'.

And quite literally, the word 'integrity' comes from the Latin word 'integritas', which means wholeness.

So what I'm really saying is this: That in order to have a greater sense of well being, to live a happy and Intentional Life and to form and cultivate long-lasting and genuine connections, we must be authentic and live daily with integrity and vulnerability. Basically, realise that it's cool to be you and just be yourself, true to your beliefs and values.

In our fast-paced society, we can often take shortcuts that compromise our integrity. We then end up feeling misaligned with our values. As we pursue an Intentional Life, slowing things down and living the life we truly desire, let's work through some exercises to fully connect with our values and live with more integrity.

EXERCISE 1

- Revisit your values from Chapter 7.
- Do you need to revise any of them?
- Note them down here.

EXERCISE 2

- What do you need to do, or change, to bring your values and your integrity into alignment? Think about how you will behave, think and feel.
- What do you need to consciously do every day to live with integrity?

EXERCISE 3

You know I love accountability! (See next the chapter!)

- Find an Integrity Accountability Partner. As always, having someone to regularly check in with to ensure that you are consistently showing up authentically in your life, is one of the best tools. This is a friend or Coach who you can run through scenarios or blocks with in order to ensure that you are living in alignment with your values and living with integrity.

CHAPTER 15

ACCOUNTABILITY

As a Life Coach I'm all about accountability. It's one of the many tools I support my clients with. When I'm working with my clients, we always set goals and dates to keep them focused and accountable and moving forwards. You know how it is. You're more likely to go to that evening yoga class if you promised a friend you would go together, than if you go on your own.

Accountability helps us take personal responsibility for our goals, our lives and of course our happiness. In the words of author Elizabeth Gilbert, speaking on Oprah's Super Soul Sunday: *'Things didn't start changing for me until I took 100% accountability for the care of my own soul. Which is to say — 100% accountability for my own life.'*

So here are my 3 accountability steps:

1. **Take personal responsibility.** In order to lead a

proactive and Intentional Life you must take personal responsibility for cultivating your best life. Living an Intentionally Happy life won't happen by luck, by winning the lottery or because other people appear to have it easier. It will come through clarity, self belief, being proactive and keeping accountable.

2. **Set clear, specific and timed goals.** Research by the American Society of Training and Development found that you have a 65% rate of success in completing a goal when you are accountable to someone. With an accountability partner and with specific goal dates, that rate of success increases to 95%.

   Gail Matthews has also conducted research on accountability and goal setting. She found that writing down your goals, publicly committing to them and accountability has a positive impact on achieving your goals.

3. **Garner lots of support**. Find your tribe. An accountability partner. A coach or a mentor. Find like-minded people who encourage and support you. Join a group for your goal. It's what got me to complete this book! I have many people in my life that keep me accountable and on track. Everything from my nutritionist keeping me accountable for my

diet, my book group so that I finish a book on time or my mastermind groups that make sure I move forwards in my business.

EXERCISE

- Make a list of the people in your life who can become your accountability partners and reach out to them.
- Make a list of the people/groups/professionals you need to keep you accountable and put that support in to place.

And of course, if you want to have accountability, support and motivation from other like-minded people as you work through the steps to Intentional happiness, then join me in the Intentional Happiness Circle.

http://julieleonardcoaching.com/intentional-happiness-course/

PART 3

CHAPTER 16

MOVING FORWARDS

Congratulations! You did it! How do you feel? Now you are clearer on the life you wish to lead, have goals that you have set and are making progress on. I sincerely hope that you are focused and consciously working on your happiness every day. I hope you feel excited with the anticipation for the life you are cultivating. Above all, I hope you feel happier.

In the Intentional Happiness Circle we cover a topic per month. The full programme takes one year, after which people carry on working through the steps over and over again.

Your happiness is a constant journey so keep checking in through the steps. Regularly review your vision for your life, what goals you need to revise or new goals to set., Check that they are in alignment with your values, make time and space to work on them and keep your focus.

You now have the proven life-changing steps to live an awesome life! Go rock your life!

ACKNOWLEDGEMENTS

Thank you Wendy Andrew for being my accountability partner every step on this book-writing journey. For the endless calls, WhatsApp chat and cheering me on over the months. You made this experience even better by sharing it with me.

Emee Estacio, thank you for inviting me into your Get It Done Challenge and for your support, encouragement and for generously sharing all your knowledge with me.

My deep appreciation to Sara Janasz for your editing and thoughtful suggestions on how to improve my manuscript.

Wendy, Nadine and Gillian, my Beta Readers. Thank you for your time, feedback and unfaltering support and friendship.

Ginny Krauss, thanks for always believing in me and for the How To Rock Your Life title. You know me so well.

And to all my family and friends who supported me during the process and read my book. I appreciate and value every single one of you.

Thank you Cristiano for your love and for always supporting me.

NOTES

https://www.hinduismtoday.com/blogs-news/hindu-press-international/scans-of-monks--brains-show-meditation-alters-structure--functioning/4574.html

https://www.actionforhappiness.org/

Kahneman,D and Deaton,Angus High Income Improves Evaluation of Life But Not Emotional wellbeing. September 2010 Proceedings of the National Academy of Sciences 107(38):16489-93

Dweck, Carol (2017) Mindset: Changing The way You Think To Fulfil Your Potential

https://scottjeffrey.com/

Dan Sullivan - https://www.strategiccoach.com/

Rivkin, I. D., & Taylor, S. E. (1999). The effects of mental simulation on coping with controllable stressful events. *Personality and Social Psychology Bulletin, 25*(12)

Front. Psychiatry, 30 October 2019

Arbuthnott, K.D., Geelen, C.B. & Kealy, K.L.K. Phenomenal characteristics of guided imagery, natural imagery, and autobiographical memories. *Memory & Cognition* **30,** 519–528 (2002).

Skottnik, L., & Linden, D. (2019). Mental Imagery and Brain Regulation-New Links Between Psychotherapy and Neuroscience. *Frontiers in psychiatry, 10,* 779

Taylor, S. (2011). Envisioning the future and self-regulation. In M. Bar (Ed.). New York: Oxford University Press.

Taylor, S. E., Pham, L. B., Rivkin, I. D., & Armor, D. A. (1998). Harnessing the imagination: Mental simulation, self-regulation, and coping. *American Psychologist, 53*(4), 429–439.

Pham, L. B., & Taylor, S. E. (1999). From thought to action: Effects of process- versus outcome-based mental simulations on performance. *Personality and Social Psychology Bulletin, 25*(2), 250–260.

Lyubomirsky, S. (2007). The How of Happiness. London: Penguin Books

Locke, E. A., & Latham, G. P. (1990). A theory of goal setting & task performance. Prentice-Hall, Inc.

Locke, E. A., Shaw, K. N., Saari, L. M., & Latham, G. P. (1981). Goal setting and task performance: 1969–1980. *Psychological Bulletin, 90*(1), 125–152.

Doran, G. T. (1981). *There's a SMART way to write management's goals and objectives.* Management review, 70(11).

Kaftan, O. J., & Freund, A. M. (2018). The way is the goal: The role of goal focus for successful goal pursuit and subjective well-being. In E. Diener, S. Oishi, & L. Tay (Eds.), *Handbook of well-being.* Salt Lake City, UT: DEF Publishers. DOI:nobascholar.com Online:

Kasser, T. Ryan, R, M. (1994). Further Examining the American Dream: Differential Correlates of Intrinsic and Extrinsic Goals.

Jebb, A. T. Tay, L. Diener, E. Oishi, S. (2018) Happiness, income satiation and turning points around the World. Nature human behaviour.

Lee M-A, Kawachi I (2019) The keys to happiness: Associations between personal values regarding core life domains and happiness in South Korea. PLoS ONE 14(1): e0209821.

Kasser T. Materialistic values and goals. Annu Rev Psychol. 2016;67:489–514. pmid:26273896,

Schmuck P, Kasser T, Ryan RM, Intrinsic and extrinsic goals: Their structure and relationship to well-being in German and U.S. college students. Soc Indic Res. 2000,

Kasser T. (2000) Two versions of the American dream: Which goals and values make for a high quality of life?. In: Diener E., Rahtz D.R. (eds) Advances in Quality of Life

Theory and Research. Social Indicators Research Series, vol 4. Springer, Dordrecht.

Hellevik, O. Economy, Values and Happiness in Norway. *Journal of Happiness Studies* **4**, 243–283 (2003).

 https://positivepsychologynews.com/news/derrick-carpenter/20070222123

https://en.wikipedia.org/wiki/Time_management

Cirillo, Francesco(2018) Pomodoro Technique- The Life Changing Time Management System

Kondo, Marie (2014) The Life Changing Magic of Tidying

Chandra, Sheila (2010) Banish Clutter Forever: How the toothbrush principle will change your life.

https://hackspirit.com/personal-development-goals/

Yerkes, R & Dodson, J. - "The Dancing Mouse, A Study in Animal Behavior" 1907 "Journal of Comparative Neurology & Psychology", Number 18, pp 459–482

Csikszentmihalyi, Mihaly. (1990). Flow: the psychology of optimal experience. US. Harper Row.

https://www.viacharacter.org/character-strengths

Matthews, G. Dominican University of California. https://www.dominican.edu/sites/default/files/2020-02/gailmatthews-harvard-goals-researchsummary.pdf

Brown, Brené (2018) Dare To Lead: Brave Work. Tough Conversations. Whole Hearts.

https://www.reddit.com/r/getdisciplined/comments/1q96b5/i_just_dont_care_about_myself/cdah4af/

https://medium.com/@fayadh56/the-concept-of-no-more-zero-days-and-why-motivation-is-fleeting-9c1c307f8948

https://www.lifehack.org/382332/what-does-procrastination-your-happiness

https://www.facebook.com/GilbertLiz/photos/710556985693086

ABOUT THE AUTHOR

Julie Leonard is a Certified Life Coach and Happiness Evangelist with 30+ years of Psychology, Health and Coaching Experience. In addition to her Coaching practice, she is also the founder of Sunndach (an online coaching programme) http://sunndach.com/portal, the creator of The Intentional Happiness Circle http://julieleonardcoaching.com/ and author of The Daily Happiness Moment Journal. She is also the host of the monthly online International Happiness Club.

Julie is passionate about happiness and living life with intention and supporting women to feel happy. She truly believes that you do not have to be defined by your past, held back by your limiting beliefs or remain stuck because of your negative inner critic and fear.

She used to be that woman. But not anymore, and not for a long time. After transforming herself and her life and supporting over 1000 women, she knows that you can take control of your life, let go of limiting beliefs, get clear on what you want and truly live the life you desire. To be successful. To be Intentionally Happy.

Find out more about Julie and her work at
http://julieleonardcoaching.com/

Join her Happiness Club at
https://www.facebook.com/groups/HappinessClubVIP/

And follow her on Instagram:
Julie Leonard (@julieleonardcoaching)

THE INTENTIONAL
HAPPINESS CIRCLE

What Participants Of The Intentional Happiness Circle say:

'I think that in order to have a meaningful life you have to work on being intentional. I was part of Julie's Intentional Women's group for a year and it was amazing. She helped build awareness in topics where I did not think to think about. I loved the exchange between the ladies in the group. True transformation happens when you have a great coach, but also when the student puts in the work. Julie rocks! I highly recommend her group program to anyone who wants to live more intentionally and is ready for more!'

'It has been a pleasure to be part of Julie's Intentional Living Group this last year, and I can't recommend this group enough. Julie's positive nature, can-do attitude, and ability to teach simple strategies that lead to big changes has allowed me personally to grow as an individual and start using everyday strategies to live intentionally and bring more joy into my life. The group provided

additional support and accountability that proved to be invaluable to my journey. I highly recommend working with Julie as she truly brings light and positivity to all the lives she touches.'

"Intentional happiness at first felt so out of reach for me at that point in my life. I was an overwhelmed mom, entrepreneur, and new mom to my second child. I was in a season of putting everyone else around me first, and myself and my soul last. I knew that something had to change, and that is when Julie invited me to learn more about Intentional Happiness and how I could be in control of changing my everyday life. The tools and lessons she taught me have been some of the most valuable lessons I have ever learned. I took the practices to heart, and loved how most were simply 5-10 minutes in my day – it felt manageable. Wow, it's now been almost three years and my life has been completely changed from who I was then, and the lessons are those I am practicing every day, and it has helped me achieve so much intentionality in all areas of my life. I am forever grateful for Julie, her work, and the effort she takes to truly share it with those of us who need it, right when we need it most."

'Julie Leonard has been a guiding light for me. Her calm and caring demeanour always puts you at ease. Taking part in her Intentional Living Group and the Intentional Happiness Club has given me concrete tools and guidance to refer and work with when I am struggling. I would highly recommend Julie time and time again!'

I open up the Intentional Happiness Circle once per quarter. Book here to get on the waitlist

http://julieleonardcoaching.com/intentional-happiness-course/

Printed in Great Britain
by Amazon